elsewhere

by Dawson Cobb

ISBN: 1453804579
ISBN 13: 9781453804575
LIBRARY OF CONGRESS CONTROL
NUMBER: 2010913397

for my Jim

CONTENTS

The Upper 2%
Barbaro
Single Song
Beacon
Train
Identity
Finale
Missing Man

Wayfarer
The Ocean
Sand
Past Presence
Time
Shadows Were Shadows
Exquisite Cliff
Apocalypse
Awake
Cadence
Disturbance
Microcosm
Philadelphia
New York City
Venite
Distractions
Wind

Ether
Press Conference
Quest

The Bear
Opening Night
Success
Bubbly Carriage
Cinders and Tin
Six Word Stories

Escapee
The Wild Beast
Process
Dawn*
At the Brandywine
Masterpiece
Unheralded
For Pearl*

PROLOGUE

Ideas scatter
on simple sunless days.

Thoughts mine the earth.
Failure glares,
and hope drags far behind.

Destinies bumble by
and tomorrows come
one by one.

i. strange lands

One brave old tree...

ONE DAY IN PARIS

The Louvre is closed on Tuesdays.
Rain is on the windshield
and scaffolding on the
Arc de Triomphe.

Fountains with lacy spurts
splash in contest
with unassuming,
      unrehearsed,
      unrelenting
          rain.

Snorting motorcycles
sever traffic undaunted;
sidewalk vendors shut and lock
and scurry off;
the Seine churns,
but continues
when it rains in Paris.

Petite cars run amok;
we side-step French puddles,
and derring-do umbrellas,
then we discover:

Notre Dame with its wobbly candles
welcomes pilgrims in from the rain
on Tuesdays.

Musee d'Orsay
with splendor and glass
invites people in,
(no trains allowed)
on Tuesdays.

The Eiffel Tower
receives guests
in the rain
      (except for dogs).
With cast iron impudence
and noisy black cables,
it pulls us to the top,
and all of Paris
unfolds
beneath us
on Tuesday
in the rain.

LONDON

Big Ben measures time behind fog.
Four bronze lions guard the square.
The blind stone lion leads us.
Red buses grunt, small taxis snicker.

London's craggy old buildings still remember.
Kensington Palace has a special ghost.
London's history is orderly romantic confusion.
Strangely, I didn't notice the trees.

The British smash syllables so eloquently.
Londoners are a lost, hurried bunch.
So few English are prim and proper.
In Bloomsbury there was waiflike rhetoric.

All English air belongs to Shakespeare.

PONTE VECCHIO

The last time
there was trouble in Florence,
enemy warriors decided
this bridge too beautiful to bomb.
Buildings were assaulted
on either side,
but the bridge stood.
Created by 9th century Romans,
there had been floods and fires
and battles in between.
(Too beautiful, perhaps, but
strong enough for tanks
to grumble across.)

Now, it sells silver, gold
and gems of all sorts.
Some tourist photographs
are taken.

SAMURAI

I stand guard
on the black bridge

watching a horse
in a silver harness

pull the wooden carriage
across to the other side.

Clear water careens over stones
racing with itself toward infinity.

Cranes scoop the air
just above the mountain.

At the urging of wind,
willows whisper.

The horse comes back,
his carriage empty.

I stand guard.

MINATO-KU, TOKYO

I walk the dogs
in morning
darkness
among embassies
and diplomatic
ghosts.

No trace
of previous
war.

No planes
droning overhead
on zulu time.

Raucous crows
instead,
meander above
the morning.

One brave
old tree
listens.

PLACES

In the weakest of moments,
I decided to travel:

Paris was architecture,
romance and rain;

London posed
with royalty and rain;

Rome had scattered beauty
with too much painful history;

Tokyo was a smug hurly-burly,
everyone moving in tandem.

I returned to the prairie:

    flowers on the edge,
    not as much water,
    more peace,
    a place to wander
            and empty the mind,
    a place to savor the scarcity
    of one's fellow man,
    a place where
    sidewalks and strangers
    don't matter.

ii. someone

...shall I call?

DIFFERENCE

I am in the city,
you are on the plains.

I have orchids on my balcony,
you have sunflowers with weeds.

I market herbicides,
you do only organic.

I drive a car from Germany,
you, a hybrid from Japan.

I have a French Bull Dog,
you, a Border Collie.

I read the *Wall Street Journal*,
you, the *Farmers' Almanac*.

Is the prairie as lonely
as they say it is?

I could change that.

EVERYTHING

You are
my *Sunday Times*
alfresco,
rare cheese
on porcelain,
early fog
touching trees,
warm sand
Nantucket, Nice.

You are
my map
for distant places,
chimes that tell
the hour,
my amulet,
my talisman,
platinum
with precious stone.

You are
my walking stick
for rocky paths,
umbrella
for sudden showers,
street lamps,
stained glass,
and compass
(for this lost soul).

SOME RAINY SUNDAY

I've never loved you.
I think you're boring.
Your view of the river
can't compare with mine.

Your tattered bearskin rug
sprawls over splinters.
Orientals adorn my parquet.

Your English Bull Dog hates
my Persian, my Russian Blue.

Your Wyeth could never
mix with my Klee.

...but when Bob,
and Sam and Clement,
George and Harry
are away...

shall I call?

Perhaps if it's Sunday,
and it's raining.

I'll bring the Campari.

I know the way.

LEGEND

I still have trouble
reading maps.

There is an ocean
between us now.
How I love
every sloshing
wave of it!
(Fathoms are
superbly deep.)

Deserts have separated
us too,
each grain of sand
sufficiently large.

Sharp and silent
mountains were there
when we needed them:
blank at the top,
sheltering trees below.

The plains were best,
occasional purple flowers,
unflappable black cows grazing,
cornfields blurring past
the windows of our train.

I remember your eyes…
blue, I believe.
Your touch nurtured
once or twice.

POSTCARD

You are someone I've seen before.
Was it the night train to Venice,
or a ski slope at Klosters.

I remember the fit of your clothes,
and the way you moved.

I wondered about your world,
your children, your dog,
or if you had a horse
with a barn.

Maybe you're an illusion,
a picture postcard
from some far-off land,
perhaps an actor
posing on and off stage,
trying to please faceless
crowds.

Don't leave
until morning.

CRUMBS

In my little cup, it is warm.
A small Madeira napkin
is my blanket,
a bit of scone,
my pillow.

The room is drafty:
a candle flame wavers,
then, sputters out.

Footsteps snap
across the porch,
and fade into darkness:
someone was here.

A someone whose love
is measured
with demitasse spoons.

A someone who
steadfastly leaves
only crumbs.

EARTHLINK

This first son
of a first son,
this Roman numeral
three,
in his polyester
and paper
underpinnings,
scrutinizes
embroidered airplanes
on his size zero to six
pastel pants.

This mortal
in miniature
inspects,
caresses,
squeezes.
He squints
and peers
and sneezes
while a Teddy Bear
with toes looks on.

When this small human
cries,
it is with a gusto
that shakes the ceiling
and resonates
room to room,
caused by some
private travesty,

a war within,
a serious anger
from ages past.

But when he laughs,
a distant treasure
bubbles;
he grins
with nodding chuckles
in unabashed,
unguarded,
glee.

We latch him in
his infant swing
and wind it up.
He's catapulted
back and forth;
he's nonchalant,
blasé in his automated
new world.
Sifting baby data,
rehearsing future plans,
he looks at his feet
in smug anticipation.

I ponder his genetics.
Will his blue eyes
be laced
with ice crystals?
Will he drink
his coffee black?
Western Kansas
trembled from outlaws

who bore his middle name;
there is Pennsylvania
and Oklahoma;
his coat-of-arms
is chequered.

I buckle this baby
close to me
in his canvas pouch.
We go for walks.
I whisper all my wisdom.

I whisper several prayers.

VISITOR

A simple cabernet will do.

I heard the woodpecker this morning.

A table in the garden is fine.

What is the weather?
Are there some clouds?

Dandelions cannot be happening!

Do we have any Camembert?

Where is the cat?
Has the dog had his bath?

Make sure the garage door is closed.

iii. etc.

... or even piano at the Carlyle.

THE SOMEDAY GAME

Does the river
still flaunt
its indolence;
or is it flowing
with assorted bits
of orphaned wood?

Do the
winds still come
as quick as death?

Does the flagpole's chain
in the school yard
still clink?

Do puddles
still quiver
at their newness?

Do posters
(on leaning poles)
still tell of circuses
that are, by now,
in some other town?

Do they back there,
those who stayed
while we smugly left,
do they still play
the someday game?

We are labyrinths
older now.
Time has etched
us gently.

Let's go back,
you and I!
Let's see
what has gone on.
Shall we trade them
An ocean for a river?

STEEP

And I suppose
there is a place
for me to go
and hide my face.

A place to go
and say my prayers
or knock on wood,
or take on dares.

There is a place…
but on a hill
where paths
can twist
and hunters
kill.

SOLOIST

The bird in our backyard was better
than goings-on at the Opera House,
or even piano at the Carlyle.
He began to sing at the earliest dawn
and was still robust after dark.
(There was no intermission.)
His fortissimo helped spring to begin
and encouraged summer along.

Suddenly we missed his melodies;
we didn't notice what day or time.
Our garden went unheralded.
Spring and summer arrived a cappella.
Small groups of chirpy also-rans auditioned,
but there were no more crescendos....

Where does a bird go,
when the song is finished ?

RUSH HOUR

Elan strolls up the boulevard.

Ennui waits for the light.

Chaos rides a cab uptown.

Calamity crosses the bridge.

Fiasco takes the tunnel.

Failure sits on the curb.

Decision takes the train.

It's beginning to rain.

PERMISSION

Watch the violence,
kick your brother,
but don't leave crumbs.

Play in traffic,
talk with strangers,
but don't leave crumbs.

When you are older,
and lost in the forest,
then, leave crumbs!

HALF EMPTY, HALF FULL

We were looking for a summer place
in the Berkshires.
At the end of an uncertain pebbly driveway,
high up on Washington Mountain Road,
a small cottage leaned,
the porch roof posed at a slant
as if squinting its critique
of us as buyers.

The splintery front door was partly open,
its screen whimpered at our approach.
We stepped onto a warped squeaky floor,
the kitchen.
A bottle of Four Roses whisky, half empty, half full
stood on the beige linoleum countertop.

We went up the steep stairway
into the only bedroom.
Jagged pieces of wallpaper dangled:
vague floral, stubborn pastels.
The ceiling had stains,
recalling raging cloudbursts, no doubt.
The double bed was made perfectly,
a pale blue chenille bedspread presided.
The only closet had a single dress,
petite and nicely pressed,
the lone memento.

This house, so haunting in broad daylight,
must be trying after dark.

We left, the bottle still there,
half empty, half full.

I wondered about ice.

BOREDOM

While I straighten pictures
and make pots of tea,
I read Mrs. Woolf
and think about me.

I listen to March winds
press windows and door,
while hours flatten
across the floor.

I smoke small cigars,
have red wine with cheese
and when morning comes,
I do as I please.

THE UPPER 2%

A rich man's sport--
something to do,
when there is nothing to do,
even the mounts are bored.
The costumes are
expensively pastel.

When the match is over,
(half past the edge of Newport),
tired horses are led
back to the stables.
Cocktails are served,
poseurs clink each other's glasses,
and conversations become
pennants waving in the breeze
on the club porch.

Is there a rumble
of restlessness
among the game players,
or is it just the boredom
the ponies
already know?

Waiters, wearing starchy white jackets
that never reveal envy,
move in rhythm
with the solemn afternoon.
They surgically carry trays;
the drinks are never spilled.

BARBARO

His stall is empty,
the stable quiet...

Will Seabiscuit welcome him?
Will St. Francis bring him hay?

Races will be easier now,
(the sky is his new track).

Those wings will take
some getting used to.

SINGLE SONG

There is a peaceful misery
that happens after war:
staccato bullets stop;
artillery shells don't echo;
bombers silently disappear
behind clouds.

On a distant
broken tree,
one bird
sings.

BEACON

This quiet warrior
was late,
when a wavy sea change
washed away
his cross-cut courage...

Did he notice
his samurai sword
left a mark
across the sand?

The literal sunrise
splashed through
the camouflage haze,
which reminded him
to look beyond
the lighthouse.

TRAIN

A far-off whistle
warns the horizon
about a train traveling
along the dimming sunset,
listening for bells
at each small town,
defying the dusk,
whistling away the unknown;
it targets the darkness
with a single light
pulling tank cars, box cars,
cattle cars...
crusading across the plains
where covered wagons
went before.

IDENTITY

There is a maze
that I wander
in wilderness,
on mountainsides,
with tossing ships,
under vacant moons.

There is a place
I used to live
before this grand
confusion came.
I wonder who is
there right now.

I wonder if
she knows
her name.

FINALE

Will it come in the night quietly,
or during the glare at noon?
Will it come with thunder
and lightning
or from battle's gaping wound?
Will it be violent,
will it be calm,
or will it be so unexpected,
there won't be time for a psalm?
How soon 'til we miss
billboards and neons?
Assuming someone sobs,
will we hear?

And like a sea of dandelions
along the wind, we disappear.

MISSING MAN

With a harsh roar
one plane swerves off
without warning and
with precise elegance
stabs the sky;

dares the clouds;

flaunts lonely courage.

The formation
pretends not to notice
and continues whistling
past the graveyard.

The sky swallows.

A hero rests.

iv. universe

... swimming in the glue of context.

WAYFARER

There is banter over cocktails
about doomsday.
There is rumor of war,
and the dance music fades.

My thoughts roll around
like marbles on a dirty floor.
The planet apparently still spins.

There is rain with dark clouds
and strong wind;
hail, shot from icy guns,
bangs the porch roof.

But somewhere, off in the distance
there is music, again,
and I begin to dance.

THE OCEAN

The ocean is on the edge of town;
its churning can be heard at the tavern.

The ocean has history underneath.

Mouldering sailors wait for rescue,
(they can't hear the ocean's indifference).

After that famous quarrel with the ice,
sodden Gladstones lie on the ocean floor.

Maps show treasure chests forgotten by pirates,
hidden by the ocean, but still on the minds of many.

Down below there are schooners from centuries past,
no longer waiting for the wind.

The ocean is too wet for waging war,
except for German submarines.

The ocean can't decide whether to be placid
or stormy, romantic with starlight reflecting,
or ominous with mysterious containment.

Until the ocean decides,
it continues to slap the shore,
and we stay in the tavern, listening.

SAND

Some people prefer the shore.

No one mentions the sand.

Do they notice
how smug the ocean is?
(It brought over the Mayflower.)

Do they know
it's in cahoots with the moon?
(Or so the charts say.)

Alongside the waves
there are many shells
containing very small ghosts.

And sometimes the waves
wear splotchy fog
that always hides something.

Then there's that flat horizon
that goes to the very edge,
cutting the sky straight across.

PAST PRESENCE

A jagged fragment
from some neighboring galaxy
sidestepped pesky black holes,
borrowed other orbits,
heedless of history to come,
careened from aeon to aeon.

Then there were monotonous waves,
too much sand,
muffled music,
laughing children,
collectors...

Now,
in a beach house
at Brewster,
on Cape Cod,
a small smooth
paperweight sits
on a writer's desk.

TIME

somewhere

amid thistles

and magic

there is a road

leading

from the edge

with no

boundaries

or stop signs

only rolling fields

knowing clouds

scattered cows grazing

everyone waiting

everyone waiting…

SHADOWS WERE SHADOWS

When everything was in black and white,
life was so much simpler:
shadows were shadows
and nothing more,
our sky was uncluttered,
trolleys clanged,
church bells echoed routinely,
trains circled mountains
and chugged across prairies,
tractors stumbled over fields
of family farms,
black smoke climbed
from factory chimneys
unfettered.

Then Wall Street fell like broken glass,
and dust smothered the plains.
Overseas, an era of ashes and rubble
began.

Years blundered along.
No one noticed---
until like a ghostly cavalry,
we emerged from the mist,
and scurried beyond the shadows
toward the faltering frontier.

EXQUISITE CLIFF

The shimmering spectre
was standing
in stunted madness,
while twilight grazed
the mountain,
avoiding
glowing icicles,
wanting
hammering sunshine,
and sighed
when the solar system
laughed.

APOCALYPSE

Just as our earth
was vibrating with spring,
the sky fell.

A chicken had warned us.

Survival became important;
fleeting madnesses
were cast aside;
suddenly every path had brambles;
there were no detours;
we longed for mindless
merriment.

Then we met
the chicken again.
This time,
its warning had
changed
to laughter.

AWAKE

Speeding lights
intrude through
the parted drapes,
sliding across the ceiling,
in rhythm with the night.

Flashing red lights
and sirens that pierce,
slice the room
into even pieces,
reminding me
someone, somewhere,
is a beat closer
to oblivion
than I am.

Stars and moon upstaged,
I lie there,
wondering...

How dark
can darkness be?
When is blackness
black enough?
How much
is too much?

Abruptly,
dawn comes,
certainly invited
but unannounced,
framing the window;

waiting for it
can be wearing.

CADENCE

As time marches on,
the snare drums
begin to annoy me.
The drum major
faces front,
turns around, then
repeats it all over again;
his silly tall hat
has feathers
or is it fur?
Wood winds whine
across the crowd.

I am part of this parade,
but I am like the horses,
confused, wishing to be elsewhere.

Oh, to be like the brass
that punctuates the city blocks,
leaving echoes on the air!

DISTURBANCE

A corner of the sky darkens.

Tiny rapiers of rain
come straight down.
The wind's twisting sword
slashes the air, filling it
with twigs and branches
and anything else
that gets in its path.

Cows in the pasture
know about storms;
they cluster and lie down
under the big tree,
blasé in their wisdom.

Chickens scatter clucking
and screeching in to the barn.

Jack rabbits disappear
in to the brush.

No one knows where
the birds go.

A red combine trembles
while the new tractor
stands firmly by the fence,
appearing silvery soft
under snippets of light.

The whirling roar leaves
in counterpoint with
crackling glass.

Then cows get up
and resume grazing
in the wet
and flattened grass.

Silence comes,
more slowly now
than when it left.

MICROCOSM

In the dimmest
corner of my mind,
chaos swims
in the glue of context.

Obligations picnic
while duty plays cards.
Awareness meanders
along the edge
of the forest.

Complete with booming drums,
even in the rain,
a parade of distractions marches by.
No one is in step.

Our galaxy observes.
The cosmos takes note.

PHILADELPHIA

It was a woodland,
that became a city.

This is the place
where the vision
of patriots
staggers our modern
crabgrass mind.

Each street and alley
throbs with history.
The landmarks
recite chapters.
There are ghosts
everywhere.

Sculptured elegance
is at ease with
scattered new chic.
Solemn colonial poses
along cobblestone.
Greek revival punctuates.
There is shabbiness next to
old world order--they touch.

We are guided
on tours and have
some guilt at not
remembering more.

We have uncertain
stirrings inside,
while we hear
of leadership
in its purest form.

And we wish
they were here now:
the founders, the signers,
the statesmen, the craftsmen.

We emerge convinced
we are invincible,
and plan to bring
the grandchildren.

NEW YORK CITY

Cars thread through traffic:
(some impudent with loud music).
Drivers dodge delirious cabs, and
nearly graze snorting buses.
Occupants resemble crash-test dummies,
stoic in their own hollowness.

On sidewalks:
a mosaic of moving faces
reflects in store windows
while each street and alley
witness crowds pressing
in counterpoint
with echoing aloneness,
weaving a tapestry of human hurry.

Scattered puzzle pieces of sky linger.
Occasional steeples stand by.

Tall watchful buildings
wait.

VENITE

For purposes of hiding
under countless Gothics
we are absolved...

like smug gargoyles
plunging forward,
going to the same nowhere,
staring with scales and feathers
upward with sooty eyes,
dreaming alabaster dreams,
surly with wooden thoughts,
but breathing holy air!

What else is better
(for purposes of hiding)
when nothing is left
but darkness.

DISTRACTIONS

Half noticing the morning,
I moved along in mist,
although the sun was bright,
and leaves were turning.

Half noticing the morning,
like a dinghy,
I was pulled relentlessly,
leaving only small ripples.

Half noticing the morning,
the day's momentum
swept me ashore.
I felt the cold sand,

then time moved on
and left me there...

Half noticing the morning.

WIND

Does it follow a map?
Does it have a worthy destination,
or does it just go on occasional sprees
along coastlines and trailer parks
with baleful disregard for new buds
timidly trying to blossom,
or new branches trying bravely
to resist relentless power?

Sometimes,
it picks up houses, cars and belongings.
Then, it goes away
absently aiming toward the horizon,
arrogantly forgetful of what just happened.

Then breezes, romantic and refreshing,
touch us with their soft presence.
As if that's enough to help us
forget.

v. make-believe

... the Shinto gods are no longer laughing.

ETHER

We ride an imaginary substance
on this unworldly path,
out toward the stars and the planets,
traveling in rarefied air.

We watch for companion spirits,
stumble over radio waves,
pass by dogged thunder,
and side-step unruly lightning.

We must go farther
in to the upper reaches of space,
where time doesn't measure us,
and our view at long last
is unbridled.

PRESS CONFERENCE

It is not true,
I did not do it.
(It made the paper.)
I simply was not there.
I was in the barn
spinning beautiful webs.
Webs I use to catch
unsuspecting bugs;
I nibble on them
at my leisure.
My best spider thoughts happen
while I gaze on my webs
and munch away.

Life is not easy.
My eight legs get tired
trekking up fence posts
and splintery barn sides
in search of good corners
for my breathtaking webs.
The work is geometric silver and grey,
depending on the sun's whereabouts:
it is artistry that can withstand
wind and rain or whatever
the day may bring.
(Webs shimmer in the dew, you know!)

But back to the rumor.
I did not sit down beside her.
I just say "no" to curds and whey.
What is a tuffet anyway?
(This all has been so absurd,
like a fable,
or even a nursery rhyme.)

Are there any more questions?

I'm going back to the barn.
There's always mending to do.

QUEST

The rabbit's clown
looked for the ghost.
Was he lost in the lavender?
Did he go for a stroll
amid sunflowers
when the mistral began?
Would the werewolf know?
Why is this glorious goblin
not traceable?
If only he were
wearing a chip.

THE BEAR

Big Foot and I have coffee together
when we can find a thermos.
Photographers come nearly every day.
Their wheezing lenses annoy me, and
they don't bring picnic baskets.

Nature magazines can't get enough of me,
Big Foot and I laugh when they whisper,
"...try not to anger the bear".
If they only knew Big Foot lives
in the woods nearby.
What a scoop that would be!
But they can't see him:
they're busy with me.
I don't know why.
I'm not Smokey. I won't wear a hat,
and I'm not in danger like the bears up North.

There--we hear that whispering again,
"...try not to anger the bear".
Big Foot giggles,
"I think they're afraid of you".
"Not enough" I whisper,
with a little growl.

OPENING NIGHT

The stage is not swept,
the curtain is frayed
and the footlights
blink on and off.

The stage manager
is a giraffe.
He bumps his head
on the lights above.

The conductor is a frog
blurting small whispers
untranslatable,
(he's wearing black tie).

Naked crickets make up
the orchestra.
The composer is ignored.
The score has been changed,
(all is in minor key).

The lyrics are unrecognizable.
T.S. Eliot punctuated
by squawks at each octave,
since the cast is entirely of crows.

Meerkats are in line
on the front row,
listening for cymbals to clang.

Fluttery bats are in the balcony
waiting to be seated.

A big sober owl
rests in the rafters,
hoping for a denouement.

Border Collie ushers
happily greet everyone
(except the Pit Bull).
They seat him near
the rear exit;
he doesn't seem to mind
and pretends to peruse
his PlayBill.

When the curtain falls,
what will the critics say?

SUCCESS

There is a legend:
if a koi can swim
to the top of a waterfall,
it will become a dragon.

I was a very small koi
when I heard this story.
I lived in the moat around the palace,
a waterfall was in the back.
So I practiced everyday—
all through Cherry Blossom time
and the rainy season.

There were times
during my struggles
with the splashing water,
I thought I heard
the Shinto gods laughing.

Then one day, I did it:
I became a dragon,
rather small, but legends
don't specify size.
In a flash, my pale gold
changed to stunning silver and black.
I had feet!
I walked on the grass.

People began to notice.

Someone told the Emperor.
He gave me a carriage
with a driver
drawn by a team
of very small horses.

Now, I sleep in the palace foyer at night
to protect the emperor's family.
The Empress gave me
a beautiful brocade blanket
and a light so she can read Bashō
to me at bedtime.

The only problem remaining:
I must learn to snort fire.
Finding a place to practice
is hard since I don't want
to scorch the flowers.

So when you come to Tokyo,
do visit the palace;
you'll see just above the moat,
near the top of the inlaid black stones,
a carriage with handsome horses,
and I'll wave to you from the window.

My driver tells me
the Shinto gods
are no longer
laughing.

BUBBLY CARRIAGE

The brazen bullet
was a painful phase.
A stolid tree looked on.
The magenta giraffe
often mentioned
the Prince had
had a dastardly outcome.

What costly duress
happened across
the purple pasture?
Was that when
the nobleman,
usually moribund,
suddenly became
sparkling?

CINDERS AND TIN

With a clumpety-thump, a little chrome space ship
snuggled down in the meadow;
the hollyhocks trembled.

Out scurried a grinning small creature
with shiny green frog feet
and shiny green hands.
His face was handsome;
he wore black silk pajamas,
trimmed with small crystals.

"I think you're an alien," I said, politely.

I am, and I probably should leave;
I'm only just learning to fly...and to spy."

Boldly, I asked,
"where did you come from?"

"I come all the way from..."
then he paused, "what's more important,
where am I now?"

"Oh, you're on earth."

"I really must go," he said, suddenly sobbing.

"Why so soon?" I asked.

"Everyone knows there are missiles here,
aimed at babies, butterflies and bunnies."
His narrow shoulders shook as he cried,
"out where we fly, my spaceship and I collide
time and again with cinders and tin;
that's what happened to them;
they were planets too, just like you!"

"By the way," he said nonchalantly,
"what country is this?"
Then he saw my Hummer.
"Never mind, I know.
You have trouble building a car,
and you had a leader who was a movie star."
As he wiped away a tear,
he whispered, "do you have aspirins?"

I noticed his sad wet eyes.
He straightened his quivering little back,
and with light years of wisdom
said to me, "this is a dangerous
place."

He rambled on.
"...so in the scheme of things---
I think I hear my mother calling.
My wife is home alone.
My dog needs help to bury a bone.
Your planet is extraordinary,
it's all such a pity."

He spun around
on a tiny green heel.
He boarded his spaceship
and slammed its silver door.
He flew away,
and I haven't seen him
since.

SIX WORD STORIES

Stampeding buffalo rarely
stop for lunch.

Rampaging squirrels
took over the town.

St. Bernards drink only
good brandy.

Dead wolves howl only after dark.

Many snails now wear mail bags.

Puppies are too short to vote.

The fly on the wall left.

Bashful robots don't do the tango.

Not many Visigoths stay for supper.

Thank you for not dying yesterday.

vi. art

And where is the white dog?

ESCAPEE

There is chaos in my brain,
a collection of words
held for ransom,
waiting for rhyme,
prisoner of meter,
held hostage by classical form.

Free verse is in custody.

Imagery stagnates in solitary.

A tunnel is being dug
by my pencil.

THE WILD BEAST

Matisse,
father of Fauvism,
harnessed
by simple colors,
trapped among
twisted tubes of paint,
longed to be like
the fish he painted:
lying on plates
unrelentingly still,
or like his gold fish
romping in their fish bowl
unaware they were
sometime models.

His studio in Paris was
on the left bank of the Seine.
Outside his window,
the Cathedral of Notre Dame,
his bulwark,
with shadows and spires
and centuries of forbearance
posed amid traffic and vendors
and clouds bearing down.
Stone statues in niches
by the Rose Window
watched him;
were they also critics?
To be a civilian in wartime

complicated his despair;
he said he was like
"the drowning man who uttered
cries for help, but in a fine voice."
Did the Germans know
there was a wild beast
in the apartment above
using brushes
like "sticks of dynamite"?

He remembered Nice
or was it Tangiers
when coiled springs
of inner bedlam
caused his metal bed
to play concertos
on the marble floor.
He knew then...
the wild beast
could rest
only on canvas.

PROCESS

Gingersnaps rest on a tray
in the hallway.
A Wedgewood saucer with
curled lemon twist waits for espresso.
An empty crystal sherry glass
stands watch.

Just outside the window
lilacs are beginning to bloom.
From a Windsor chair
the orange cat watches
a squirrel scamper up the path.
The big gray dog is asleep
by the door.

There is stillness
that moves across
the leather-topped desk.

My pen breaks the silence.

DAWN*

In which corner
of the cosmos
is this orderly dispute?

Lines slowly map
sudden changes,
then pose over
uncertain blue.

There is a sunrise peering
with inexact glare
resting in an incomplete box.

A tree top intrudes
with its loyal shadow alongside.

Is this the dead-end
of forever,
or just innocent beginnings
of chaos?

* *View of Notre Dame,*
   oil on canvas, Henri Matisse

AT THE BRANDYWINE

And why is that
trite sunset
so burdensome?
Along the way,
was the rose horizon
lost?

The splintery barn
is up on the hill,
like Wyeth,
next to the clashing ship,
quite in disarray
with the squeaking cottage
among the broken weeds.

And where is the white dog?

MASTERPIECE

The brush begins
its journey across blankness
guided by unrehearsed strokes
with bristles that travel
a foreordained path.

Then, at one lower corner,
a signature,
the signal of completion.

Now, on a wall,
fenced in by a frame,
the canvas hangs,
and tells everything.

UNHERALDED

Here I am before you.
On the floor,
you
will see vagrant vessels
snarled,
a heap of jagged pieces,
atoms once again
askew.

Here I am before you,
in tandem with the dawn,
this obscure minor poet
persists,
and a bleary poem
yawns.

FOR PEARL*

There is quiet grandeur
when beeswax and oil
pose on canvas:
the lush surface
finds narrow places
on the spectrum
as vague hues
peer through.

This static abstraction
absorbs and reflects
while planes
of preoccupied colors
stand nearby.

*   *Oil and beeswax
    on canvas,
    Brice Marden,
    1970*

ACKNOWLEDGEMENTS

My debt of gratitude goes ...

to my teacher, Kathy Hubbard,
who is incredibly inspiring and has
patience that continues to amaze me;

to Suzy Wasson who never wavered
in her steadfast encouragement;

to Hannah Harbison, my
assistant and typist, whose
skill and dedication made
this collection possible.

INDEX

Cover, oil on canvas
by Jim Cobb

www.jimcobbpainter.com

Made in the USA
Charleston, SC
29 July 2011